LOVE AND CATASTROPHE

Poetry

By James Janko

Sturgeon Bay, WI: Four Windows Press

@ Copyright 2023 James Janko
Four Windows Press

All rights reserved. No part of this book may be used or republished by any means, including photocopying, recording, taping, posting, or by an information storage retrieval system without the written permission of the publisher and/or author except in case of brief quotations embodied in critical articles or reviews.

ISBN: 978-0-9991957-6-5

Cover art by Ethel Mortenson Davis

Novels by James Janko

What We Don't Talk About
(University of Wisconsin Press)

The Clubhouse Thief
(New Issues Poetry & Prose/Western Michigan University)

Buffalo Boy and Geronimo
(Northwestern University Press/Curbstone)

For Maxine & the Veterans,
for the Zuni Mountain Poets,
for Uong Chanpidor
&
in memory of
Robert Ray Boeskool & Jesse Grey

"I begin with love, hoping to end there."

—Jericho Brown

Contents

I

Morning 11
The Sea 12
Moon and Star 13
Sophomore at St. Anthony's High School 14
Farm Girl on Nine Acres (Circa 1908) 15
First Love 16
Why I Like This Boy 17
Mountain Rain in Illinois 18
Cherry Tree 19
Something Earned 20
Tal Vez 21
Perhaps 21
Dozing on a Bench at a Famous Museum 22
Peacock 23

II

Gravity 26
Friend, If I Go First 27
Late Summer Garden 28
Settling My Estate (California, 2021) 29

Ring 31
Two Words 32
Autumn Leaf 33
Altar 34
Bored by Discussions of the Writing Process, She Flies Away 35
Wind-Fishing 36

III

Edward R. Murrow Broadcasting from the 21st Century 38
Breathing Out 40
21st Century Survival Manual 41
Privilege 42
What Time Is It? 44
24-Hour Market 45
Stay for One Moment (Circa 1963) 46

IV

Kwan Yin: A Bodhisattva of Compassion 48
Laurie 49
Redemption 50
Soldier Home (Albuquerque, 2011) 51
First Light 52
Breakfast At the Border 53
North 54
Cloud Break 55

How One Boy Died in Viet Nam 56
Late-Night Scribble in Margins of Unpaid Bill 57
Survivors 58
In an Un-bombed Village 9 Kilometers Away 59

V

Malleable 61
Poet 62
Taste 63
Long Distance Runners 64
Medicine 65
Muse 66
Solstice Storm 67
Summer Evening 68
Rain 69
On the Water 70
Zuni Sunrise 71
Tree 72
Vigil 73
Tell Me If It's True 74
Equations 76
Acknowledgements 77
Praise for James Janko's Novels 78
Biography 80

I

Morning

A lighted field—
gold flower, yellow flower, sun.

The veins of her wrists, her hands—
the blue I long to kiss.

The Sea

The waves rushed in
and we had to leap,
bounding up over
the sand and rock.
I turned and saw
her white dress
in the wind,
a long dress like a sail,
and the great sea
boiling high enough
to toss a whale,
and I will remember
till I die and maybe longer
the way she sprang,
wave-like and reckless,
too young for wounds,
while over her sail rose
a brood of dark-winged gulls
between the ocean and the rain.

She found a broken shell
and held it to her ear.
No sound, she said. Nothing.
We were twelve years old.
She listened to my heart.

Moon and Star

Zuni Mountains, New Mexico

Jeremiah, age six, tells me the moon is
a ball of lightning stolen from a cloud.

We roll squash and corn in butter,
salt our blessings, and roast them on a fire.
I tell Jeremiah the moon and star that gave birth
in my blood eons ago have multiplied.
If I were to turn myself inside out,
the sky would be amazed!

Morning.
I love the sun on the piñon tree
and the small ant in the shade.
No less the one
than the other.

Does everything live and die for everything?
Maybe the poets know.

Sophomore at St. Anthony's High School

Jeremiah Azulema: "Are there angels disguised as birds and others who are angels and need no disguise?"

The nun closed the book. "I don't know," she whispered. "And don't ask the priest."

After school, he walks along César Chávez Avenue in bright sun. He kicks at dried leaves and twigs along the curb, whistles "Somebody Up There Likes Me," and glances from the world in front of his shoes to the world of the sky. High white clouds give him a sense of the sky's breadth, and its breath, too, its warm wind on his face and curling up the cuffs of his shirt and tickling his wrists. He decides most things are made of spirals, wriggly things like wrists and clouds and shoelaces and leaves and breath, and best of all a girl walking his way, a black-haired, black-eyed, Black girl swinging her arms as her lovely shadow, her face, drift by him, catch the light of the sky, and disappear.

    Look.

    This olive tree with wind-shaped branches could write our names in blue.

    The world's wriggly all over.

    Go ahead, try and stop beauty.

        Go ahead.

Farm Girl on Nine Acres (Circa 1908)

At night, in summer, in Illinois, she can smell the leaves of the corn and the earth that could not be blacker, where the prairies have no need of pipes, sprinklers, irrigation, where heaven and earth are enough, plenty, where the storms unleash thunderbolts, wind, rain, a bounty of darkness and light over the fields.

    At any hour, a girl can disappear in colors—
    the green of the corn leaves,
    the yellow of the harvest,
    the earth warm and black, laden with seeds,
    the Illinois River, dark green and gray and silver,
    the yellow-gold sun,
    the blue wind in the trees,
    the moon in the east, the borrowed gold,
    and the dark between the stars.

First Love

In twilight,
under moon and thunder
and scudding clouds,
we ran beside green corn
sprouting near the Illinois River
in the blackest soil on earth.

Breathless, we stopped to rest.
I began to love her when she whispered,
"These crickets know something of night.
Listen to them sing!"

One kiss under thunder and moon.

Why I Like This Boy

He shows as much interest in a spear of grass
as the hair on my arms,
as much interest in the valleys of rivers
as the shade of thighs.

He makes me wonder if
the light of our bodies and
the light of the earth
are the same light and
if they need each other
for seeds to grow.

Mountain Rain in Illinois

A yellow bird wakes the fields.
Squirrels leap from cottonwood to maple to—
    Woe! You see that?
    A cardinal more red than red
    just brightened the sun!

Eyes open, eyes closed, the same world.
The sweat of the Illinois River and
the sweat of the body
and the gathering of clouds.

Lightning scars on a towering cottonwood,
and underneath, in bare dirt, the writing of insects,
foot etchings, hieroglyphics, maybe messages
to scars and bark and to other walking things,
messages that will disappear when the storm blows in.

Follow the wind and the eddies of the Illinois.
Cloud mountains billow and spark.
Look—two lovers in the cattails near the river.
Green earth, shade of thighs.
A leap of lightning and mountain rain.

Cherry Tree

1. Long Rivers

The flowers open
after the cherry tree
pulls the light of the sky
into its taproot.

At the base of the trunk,
under a fold of bark,
an ant hears with her feet[1]
the sap, the long rivers
winding toward the crown.

2 Midsummer

The sun gives its sky-wide halo
    to half the world.
Sitting under the cherry tree,
a woman feels the heat of her blood
in the veins of leaves.

3. Her Lover Speaks at 4 a.m.

Blood on my tongue.
I taste some of the world,
some of you and me,
and open the blinds to darkness.
   Mouth.
   Blood.
   River.
   Woman.
Climbing the old cherry tree into the night!

---

[1] Ants do not have auditory canals. Instead, they have sensors in their feet and knees to feel vibrations in and upon the earth and—in this case—under the bark of the tree.

Something Earned

1. Early Evening

Red worms loosen the darkness under well-kept yards.
No wind tonight.
Women leaving their homes
hear movements in the earth.

Stars in the east.
Someone touches the trunk of a sugar maple,
her dress the color of leaves.
The moon creeps over the tree.

2. Morning

I work in the sun.
Sweat drips down my face, my back, and into the earth.
I will leave grains of salt behind, but some of me will rise.
The rising—you need a keen eye and a sensitive tongue to understand—
    makes the air heavier.
The body and sky are watery worlds.

3. Noon

I see someone in the high branches of the sugar maple.
I bend down and work harder
till my sweat rises to
meet her near the crown.
I know her mouth, her tongue,
and the green light around the tree.
Do I have to be as big as the sky for her?
No, but I have to be an honored guest of this warm green
that opens the folds of buds.
She has her whims.
She only wants me after I rub myself
hard against the tree.
Softness is something earned.
Same as love.
Same as rain.

Tal Vez

Maiz y luna.
    Una flor y una piedra.
      🌱   Δ
      roja   negra

Los grillos son amigables,
    una familia de cantores.

Y el agua
    cuchichea un sendero por los
      huesos
    para que los mares nos conozcan.

Ya nos ama todo?
    Tal vez los poetas sepan.

Perhaps

Moonlight and corn.
    A flower and a stone.
      🌱   Δ
      red   black

Crickets are friendly,
a family of singers.

And the water
    whispers a path through our
      bones
    so the seas may know us.

Does everything love us already?
Maybe the poets know.

Dozing on a Bench at a Famous Museum

No shape or color stays in place.
The mind, at ease,
sees more of what is and is not,
and may never find the margins
where one thing stops
and another begins,
where you are
     you
   and I am
     I
   and art is a
   mausoleum
on pedestals and in frames.

Degas' dancers in fluid lines,
gestures of water and light—
I see them best when I smell the sweat.
They are not fragile, not too strong either.
Only a certain softness can
move through mountains of marble,
steel beams, electricity,
webs of wires and walls,
floor and flesh,
ceiling and cloud.
How much of heaven is architecture?
        How much is pallet, knife, chisel?
        How much blood spill?
        How much earth, stone, bedrock?
        How much sky?
The questions multiply, go unanswered.
And we wake—if we wake—
in an uncertain light,
a gallery boundless and contained.

Peacock

For Chanpidor

How are you? he asks.
Fine, she says. And you?
He smiles and looks away.
Fine.

Birds seen through fog
could be angels or ghosts.
He wonders if she sees
more of what is,
or more of what
shape and shadow
invite her to imagine.
Maybe he can fool her,
try on peacock feathers,
strut and dance
through the fog
till beauty blinds her
and she relents—
"I must have you!"

The Lover, a biography,
censored and condensed:
Born in a backseat,
he was wingless and white.
And all he ever wanted was
to be as round as the sound
of a great bell and
to soar in a circle of light.

He meets her for coffee on a Saturday morning.
    How are you?
    Fine, she says. And you?
    Superfluous.
Her laughter makes him dizzy with happiness and hope.

He sees her
as only a lover can see her.
She is as enigmatic
as an egg or a drop
of his own blood.
Does something marvelous
happen every moment?
Watch her face.
Watch her mouth.
Look how pretty her teeth are
when they dent her lower lip
for the f of fine.

II

Gravity

As a boy running through Illinois,
racing deer, I longed to slip beyond
the boundaries of the skin,
to leap over the herd,
over cows in fields,
over Mr. Malecki's farm,
over clouds shaped like Jenny Brate
(I was too shy to speak to her),
and I flew out of my shoes
every summer of my life!

No boy ran faster through Illinois,
but a man knows more of gravity than flight,
the weight of blessings and blood,
the comfort of stones in their nests in the earth,
and the fields of light
wider than fields of Illinois corn
that may visit us, welcome us,
wherever we rest or wander
in the flesh of the world.

Friend, If I Go First

I could be wrong,
but this is how I see it.
We fly through the blue.
There are no ropes or wires,
nothing to cradle or clutch,
only the architecture of light,
swift and intimate,
forever a frustration
to prehensile tools.

Friend, I don't know about you,
but I must love far and wide while I can.
And all my life I'll see nothing—
mountain peak, hip bone, cloud, thigh, rainbow—
to cradle or clutch. Blessed be,
I own nothing in heaven or earth.
Friend, if I go first will you bury me naked
and plant something wild over my grave?
My last request—love me with a tree.

Late Summer Garden

They die a silent death—the flowers.
    She watches a red dahlia into the night.
It doesn't seem afraid.

Settling My Estate (California, 2021)

1

Crows, smoke—
which is darker?
Wind and fire climb
the hills to the east.
My friend's house!

My house next?

2

House, earth, sun—mortal beings.
    Language—mortal being.
Car ready to go, packed with books,
    one small suitcase.
I stagger from a dream tearing my hair—
    "Someday no one will read Shakespeare!"
My lover says, "Go back to sleep."

3

I could be bounded in a nutshell and count myself the
king of infinite space if it were not that I have bad dreams.

4

"The sun—will it really die someday?"
    "Yes, but long after you and me and our burning homes
and orange skies and roaring rivers and oceans are kaput."
        "And the words—do they have to die?"
        (I can't see who sits with me at 4 a.m., but someone seems
           to nod.)
        "The nouns, the verbs—everything?"
        "Sayonara. Try to settle your estate."

5

    I say goodbye to my house while I can,
    and to my body and my lover's body,
    mostly water and light.
    Where will everything go?
    I don't know, but I have an idea.
    Goodbye to you and me and we and
    everything but a presence—
    love without the body, the bones,
    and kindness without the word kindness.
    Is love ever squandered?
    I don't know, I don't know.
    But it's all we have while we breathe.

Ring

My mother at the jeweler's,
her hand on the glass counter.
A gnarled bone pushes against her wedding ring,
cutting off circulation.
After forty-seven years something must give—
the finger or the gold.

She bites her lower lip as the jeweler
works with his cutting tool.
Her face turns pink, now white.
Moments pass that seem like lifetimes.
The gold is removed from her hand.

An old tree on its way down
throws its last ring of light over the sun.
All else—roots, trunk, branches—
is burrowed and chewed,
a home and a pantry for small things
in the wood, the soil, the air—the feast
of a good death that spans the years.

Two Words

For Lorraine

She could live for this alone—
the early light in the oaks, the maples.
Or the darkness, too, the night alive in the creaking of joists,
maybe the nudge of roots from an old oak,
the tree and the house making adjustments,
and the scratchings in the dirt beneath the porch,
maybe a mouse, a cat, a raccoon.
She learned as a child to pray the Hail Mary,
the Our Father, and the Glory Be,
but the world taught her that two words—thank you—
can save us from wrath and greed.

She died at the age of ninety-three.
Seasons passed, and years, decades.
The letters on gravestones of St. Anthony's Cemetery
began to fade. The plastic flowers spiked to the earth
lost their glow, blended with the stone.
A slow fading away, erasure after erasure,
seemed to spread over the cemetery, over the world.
A thousand years might pass before something as
essential as a forest rises from graves, rubble.
And maybe—what lunatic would know?—
those who care for this world will pray
a simple prayer through all the years.

Autumn Leaf

A leaf, long fallen,
its surface brittle and rough,
a distant thousandth cousin
to this page I write on,
is speckled with spots,
blotches, necrosis,
though already,
in minute amounts,
it begins to lean
toward a sleeping seed
and to smaller worlds,
some of which a microscope
would reveal, and others
forever concealed
from the human eye.

One edge of the leaf
curls slightly upward,
a small disc, pale orange,
a suggestion of a rising sun.
Yet I have no wish
to give death other names,
only a longing that burns,
pale orange, as in
very hot fire,
to join and depart,
again and again,
with an equal measure
of dignity and grace.

Altar

You can say the Hail Mary,
the Our Father.
You can pray
to the sun
and the beetle
under the stone.
There is nothing
to do but pray
as the spider weaves
a beautiful death
in the new dawn,
as the worm enters
the mouth of a crow,
as the mouse
fills the sinews
of a black snake
that slides over the earth,
over blood trails, scales,
pugmarks, feathers, feet—
this mute altar of
mud and bones and light.

Bored by Discussions
of the Writing Process, She Flies Away

Not one word of death or birth,
no rivers to carry the sounds,
so she draws into herself,
the bare skin of her heart thinner than paper,
the sparrow asleep in her hand, then released.

Listen.
   Wind and wings.
   Blue light.
   Insects burrowing into graves.

Wind-Fishing

Oak branch dips, bobs,
    almost breaks—
the whole sky on the line!

III

Edward R. Murrow Broadcasting from the 21ˢᵗ Century

Skyscrapers, up to code,
    are leaning, tumbling;
the cars, the drivers, the animals, the city,
follow the steel and plaster and plastic and
rebar and glass along an upscale boulevard
and onto a freeway
that crashes into a river,
its shores crumbling and disappearing
in the sea.

Edward R. Murrow would smoke a cigarette
down to the nub,
down to three, two, one—air-time.
The gravel of his voice
suited blunt truths.

"By all accounts,
we rushed to arrive here.
Our pharaohs—I have to hand it to them—
our pharaohs make ancient Egyptian kings
look like a pack of pikers
picking through leftovers
at a second-rate picnic
beyond the gates of a burning city.
They reap what they sow:
a world reduced to an ashtray,
a shrunken head on a red stick,
an upscale boulevard tumbling to the sea.
Yes, we rushed to arrive here,
driven like cattle."
He would hesitate, turn the page,
and lower his voice to the edge of truth.
"And just think of it,
hold this thought for one moment:
All we need, all we *ever* need—pharaohs first—
    is to learn to bow.

"Good night, and good luck."

Note to readers: Please read this page from bottom to top, left to right, and rise with the Flood.

                                                    the moon."
                                                    under

       flying over the great storm and
  "Geese have never looked lovelier to the human eye
Maybe this as she treads water:
         the broken-free door of a neighbor's garage?
   as she swims for a life-raft,
What else can a girl, or even a woman, think or say on such a night
   a scream rather than a serenade."
   the Atlantic yammering and yawing,
Lord, here comes the Atlantic on a full-moon night,
   saying to herself, "The ocean's coming, the *ocean*.
Any girl who can still think in words is
   in the crown of the tallest oak for miles.
Water in Deb Madison's tree fort,
   sailing toward the sea.
Water on the deck and in the attic, old trunks
    like pretty boats on parade.
    blouses floating free of hangers and closets
    water in the basement,
Water in her upstairs' bedroom,
   fast as a teenage girl racing to her balcony to invite a serenade.
Water climbing the stairs
   now the house.
Water in the basement,

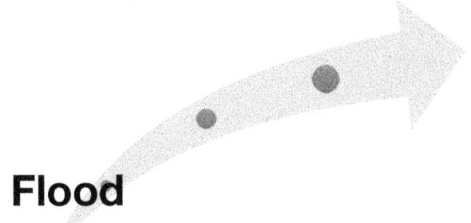

Flood

Breathing Out

People stand in line to buy water.
Fumes rise from factories, fields, and power plants.
Yet even our poison longs for something else.
Even the smoke smudging our lungs
may one day arrive again,
dark and essential,
a rain cloud over the mesa,
a shadow on a field of corn.

21st Century Survival Manual

You may live here if you see
    a moon prayer in water,
    a green root prayer in rain,
    a silverfish prayer in river,
    a monsoon prayer in the desert,
    a sun prayer in the heart of the belly,
    a fire prayer in stone,
    a shining in the air.

Privilege

It is a privilege to write and read
    to have a bed
    a roof
    a prayer
    a plate of food
    to have two arms and two legs
    to have something as complicated as a hand
    blood vessels
    a breath
    a song

It is a privilege to sit alone in a room
    pen in hand
    and write one true thing
The rewards are great, unfathomable—
    to peer beyond the cave of the skull
    to worlds larger than all of us
    to learn to yield
    to bow
    to receive
    to wait
    to witness beauty and
    sing its suggestions
    in a song
    a melody
    no two chords the same
    though echoes occur
    to offer us time to record

It is laudable
    and often essential
    to write a poem
    good or bad
    and to let the heart break
    in a broken world
    to be awake night after night
    hopeless, exhausted
(is there a place for anyone's children?)
    to sleep one hour

and wake
to disbelieve the sun
and then to glow
to belong here
right here
despite everything
in the first light of day

What Time Is It?

Sitting in forest shade, I glance at oblivion—
    the watch on my wrist.

What do the old trees know of time?
Maybe the caw of a raven flying over the mesa
helps the piñon and the ponderosa to measure the morning.
Maybe the lengthening of roots as they reach for water
speaks to the earth in languages I'll never learn.

It is 7:43 a.m. Day or night,
the watch on my wrist is a mirror,
a delicate thing,
as mortal as I am,
with light and shadow on its face.

24-Hour Market

At 4 a.m., I slump over my cart in Aisle 3.
I hear a clatter, look up,
and see a woman in black tights dancing,
cavorting this way and that
as she picks out fruits, vegetables,
showing her tap-dance moves,
her salsa and swing,
her feet swift, her wrist bracelets jangling
as she plucks red peppers, green peppers,
a mango, a purple cabbage, a yellow onion,
a red apple, a pink apple, blueberries,
and I am so happy to be alive!

Stay for One Moment (Circa 1963)

I waited in line all afternoon, all night, to file a complaint. The corridor smelled of old newspapers, cigarette butts, cigars. The woman in front of me was reading a novel, *The Seas of August*. I peeked over her shoulder to steal a few words: *Stay for one moment without imagining the rest.* I can fall in love as fast as I read.

I walked home alone. Does the first light of morning fall in love with the earth? Does it *know* it's in love? I watched a hawk glide between the domed towers of Orville's City Hall. No one in that building would understand my complaint, my language.

Stay for one moment without imagining the rest.

IV

Kwan Yin: A Bodhisattva of Compassion

Near a slow-moving river,
an old cottonwood
shades a statue of Kwan Yin
as dark and lovely as rain.
At her feet
    a yellow-white bone,
    a great arc of a bone,
the shape of a flicking and rising tail.

Kwan Yin—not the statue, but maybe anyone—
    goes into that bone,
    into that fish,
    into that river,
    into the sea,
and look how long her ears are—seven fathoms—
and how well they listen to the water-light
pouring through the mind of the world.

Laurie

1

Perhaps there are worse sins than picking wildflowers and scaring children. Pretending to know, for example. Pretending to be sure.

2

My father picked me up, kissed me, said, "See you at supper," and left for work. Car crash on Route 6. Dead. He was thirty-three, the age of Jesus. I was eight.

   Closed casket. I longed to lift the lid and watch his face till they shoved him in the ground.

3

Today I told my son about my mishap. "Danny, I accidentally slammed the kitchen door on my left hand, but it didn't hurt. The blow took my mind off the other hurt."

4

Sometimes I forget about my father when I look in my son's eyes in the near dark. I love him best when the sun goes down. He doesn't say, "Be tough, be tough." But if I were dead, I would need neither words nor their absence. Maybe just some kindness in the near dark.

5

Make a wish. We say this to children on their birthdays before they blow out candles. They receive shiny gifts moments later. I still have the red-haired doll my father gave me on my eighth birthday. I sew her seams when she comes apart.

6

My son believes in words. As if sounds and meanings could communicate a life.

   In the beginning was the Word.
   What word?
   In the end silence sifts our bones.

Redemption

It can begin this way, and maybe it has.
    A ruined man,
    solitary, repulsive, alcoholic,
    afraid to die,
is touched by a child,
    a stray hand chubby with baby fat,
    a hand—untutored, unskilled—
that opens the crumpled fist
    of a wasted mind
    in a burst of light.

The slow healing begins.
He will notice on a blue morning before he dies
    the shadow of wings
on a white chrysanthemum.

Soldier Home (Albuquerque, 2011)

Twilight in winter.
Streetlamps blink on and off.
Hiss and static and stuttered light.
Rush hour: Cars, drivers, pedestrians—
quick as sparks shooting off a grid.
I walk fast, my to-do list in a clenched hand,
till someone shakes loose the thunder of his
voice and turns me around.
"I sing for my wife! I sing for my life!"

He's young, say twenty years old,
sitting on a duffel bag, government issue.
Maybe he's back from Iraq or Afghanistan—
home but homeless. His voice, his urgency,
could snatch truth from a lion's paw.
I give him twenty cents, two dimes,
and say, "Good luck, man."
He sings again and I hear
and almost feel inside of us
the spaces we mirror and contain,
the near and far mountains, the canyons,
the wide plains, the deserts, the departed sun,
our wives and lives, the lions, the wolves,
the places where there are no snipers, no IEDs,
no rush hour, no 21st century frenzy.
Good luck? I still search my insides
for what I might have said or done to build a bridge.
I have learned well the mathematics of separation:
"Two plus two is the beginning of death."

First Light

No name, no documents,
no country worth mentioning here,
she sidles out from beneath a bridge,
peers at the sky, returns to shadows.

And less than a mile away,
in a suburb with green lawns,
the sparrows look this way, that way,
check beneath fences and over roofs
before they search for seeds buried in the earth.

Breakfast At the Border

Sunlight on her hands as she peels an orange.
Walls and razor wire rise higher than trees.
Her two children squat near a tent.

She tears her small sun with her thumbs.
If she were a tree, a god, or a revolution,
she would offer a basket of suns, turn the wire to silk.

She divides the orange between her children,
saves a slice for herself. Chewing,
sucking the juices, she walks around,
searches the bare earth for something more to share.

North

A squirrel stands on her hind legs
to peer over a snowdrift,
then wraps her tail
over her legs and feet.

I want simple words, nothing extra.
I want each one to be as useful
as a nest of warm, thick fur.
Are there words an animal or a person can eat?
Let me make a poem as hard and
bright as an ear of winter corn.
Let me make something
as useful as a walnut in a shell.

Cloud Break

Sunlight and snow
on a gray branch.
A white stripe,
warmed by claws—
red cardinal.

How One Boy Died in Viet Nam

The body is well-designed:
raise the arms to give;
make a basket to receive.

On June 6th, 1970, I walked to a well
to fill a canteen. Robert Ray Boeskool,
who wanted to pitch for the Los Angeles Dodgers
after the war, walked behind me.
The morning was bright, cloudless.
I wanted to play centerfield for the Cubs.
Did I mention this, Robert?
I see my mistake now—I forgot about death.
Sunlight and green fields, the green of rice paddies,
reminded me of far-away fields, diamonds.
It's hard to look at a ball field today.

Arms are to give and receive.
Legs and feet must move with care,
and the eyes—if I deserve them—
must search for a strand of wire
thinner than the silk spun
through the belly of a spider.
There are mistakes that last forever.
I didn't see the wire,
but I felt the tug of it on my ankle
and was thrown forward by a hot wind.
Small wounds—my left hand, my right hip.
Robert Ray bled from his eyes, throat, chest, stomach.
But he was a strong boy and took half the day to die.

Late-Night Scribble in Margins of Unpaid Bill

          one day in Cu Chi
knee-deep in paddy mush
booby trap
white flash
shards of leg
medic tying tourniquet
and hours later
REVENGE
bombs and napalm
fields and huts ablaze
no rice grass anymore
no coconut palms
no jackfruit or tamarind
no dragon fruit trees—
this is the moon
       GIs on patrol days later
leave coca cola
in dying village
show good will
win hearts and minds of ghosts
recipe for war same-same
during my time here
light the earth
shake and bake
there is a saying in SE Asia—
ants suffer when
elephants rage

Survivors

Where a great tree once stood,
small sprouts grow from a stump.
An army of ants walk over the plain
and into the forest.
They find dew,
a dozen lakes to drink from,
and maybe some sugar.
The stump with its green sprouts
and intelligent activity
and dappled shade
could be a beginning,
a continuance, or an end.

In an Un-bombed Village 9 Kilometers Away

A girl kneels in a garden,
rescues a grasshopper from a puddle.
Hop, hop—gone!
And joy shakes her awake as geese fly under the moon.

v

Malleable

Maybe we all fit in a waterdrop,
or a crack in the earth,
a sunflower seed,
or the sky clearing after an all-night rain,
or the caw of a raven,
that *blackness* as necessary as sunrise,
or the ears of a deer,
electric, alert for lions,
or the first breath of a child,
or the last,
or somewhere in between,
a slight gap,
a swerve,
invisible,
a shadow on a cliff,
a spark,
an ember,
here and gone,
maybe to return.

Poet

You can be the sky above
a tree, a twig, a leaf,
or a stone that becomes
unknowable as you
kneel for a closer look.

You can be the sky over
a poem, a story, a psalm, a song,
a weaver with pencils and moons,
sunlight and stars, and rubbed
rocks that brighten and spark—
the lightning that reads the page.

You can be the sky opening
blue arms to spread seeds and wind,
the sky that bows low
and digs in the red earth.

You can be the rain that plows the earth,
that opens the caves,
the shapes and sounds of words,
and you can be the ear, the mouth,
the language of the world,
if you are humble enough
to move out of the way and
invite the stones to speak.

Taste

In the Zuni Mountains, when I was three,
my mother showed me to the moon.
We left the night shade of a Ponderosa pine
and walked into a valley where our faces,
our muslin dresses, beige and blue, caught the light.
She took my hand and said to the moon,
"Lucky you, you have a pretty sister."
And the moon was even prettier
in the reflected light of the unseen sun.

Ice and salt—
I learned my taste when I cut my tongue in winter.
I wonder how the moon tastes in December,
or the sun in July as we turn in its light.

Long Distance Runners

Two girls, running at twilight through the shadows of the mesa,
are watched by juniper and piñon trees,
by the growing dark that shelter the deer, the elk,
the lion and her cub, and one thousand nests for birds.

The night has blessed us for eons.
And now the heavens, the first stars, the new moon,
watch over the mesa as the girls run outward in a spiral,
run faster and with little effort, perhaps tracing on the earth
an ancient pathway through the autumn sky.

Medicine

It is her silence
that calls to
the juniper and
the piñon and
the ponderosa,
the deer and
the lion and
the bear—
Come visit me.
Then the trees
and the animals
warm her throat
and swing her arms:
the singing and
the drumming begin.

Muse

I am old beyond years.
I don't see well
or hear well,
but at first light
I spot a raven
darkening a piñon tree,
I hear a circle of song.
Someone across the mesa
spins a wheel while singing
her morning prayers.
Will she visit me
before the sun is a full circle?
I write for whoever comes near.

Solstice Storm

All the trails are behind him.
In the last light of December 21st,
he climbs till he reaches a ridge,
the jutting stones of the high mesa.
A deer and two does huddle near a piñon tree.
The mother lifts her head and
her nostrils flare, quiver,
a black flower more delicate
than the steam of her breath.

A human scent means danger.
He can only nod as the mother and her young
bound over boulders and brush,
leap a stream, a gully, and disappear.

He stands as still as the piñon tree
when the snow begins.
Maybe this time he will vanish
in the mesa until the deer return,
and the elusive lion, the famished bear. He
will imitate St. Francis
until the animals believe he *is* St. Francis, or
someone else, original, unrecognizable, who
fell from a pedestal into a field of grace.
The lion may devour him,
or the bear, the tree, the mesa,
or the whole world before the sun's return.

Summer Evening

For Sayword, for Clare

The convent behind her, she walks alone near dark trees.
Crickets, katydids, a cat asleep in the grass,
and a stirring in the air of unseen birds,
bats, the swiftness of wings.

The night smells like a soft wound,
a smear of blood on willows, a cut almost healed,
or no, a deep fissure that once split the earth in warm halves.

What is this ache in the bones of her chest?

Jesus always longed to give Eucharist to forests and fields.

Rain

El Morro, New Mexico

Perched on a telephone pole,
a raven turns her back to the wind.
Due north,
over the mesa,
rain weaves and splices
sky and earth,
cloud and stone.
The raven watches me watching
and flies with the wind
as I lift my pencil and make
loops and lines on a blank page.
I begin to imitate her flight,
then pause, less ambitious,
and trace the shape of my heart.
In the desert only one sound
can improve silence.
The rain drums a storm
on my roof, more beautiful
than any rhythm or word
a writer may convey.

On the Water

My long back on the waves,
drifting with leaves and light,
I love all that goes beyond me.
I look out on the stars,
the stars look inward.
I close my eyes and
hear the silence of the earth.

Zuni Sunrise

Green pine on blue mountain.
Bird nest opens to the east—
   three yellow eggs!

Tree

                    from
         free   a branch,
   Flying   Mr. Bird?

              Thank
               the
               tree
              down
             through
               her
              roots
               and
              way
              down
              deep
              into
               the
              dark
 . ,:..:΄΄∂∫.¶ ≈'.,∞:°~:...
 .:°∞§≈...¶,∞..:∂.:.."∫.,¶.§,.∂:˙.:.
 ...§°¶ . : .' ∂.:.∞'∫.,¶≈:'§.'∂.' ∂:,∫.'¶,:.˙ ..
 ,. " ¶,   .: .,≈:., ¶ :'," ..".: .¡ ¶: "... ≈ :. ,¶..:. .

Vigil

A feral cat runs across the August fields—
orange fur, brown and yellow grass,
red ants in the shadows of stems.

Vultures circle the fringes of storm clouds.
A squirrel digs up a seed
and runs up a lightning-scarred oak.
There she sits on a green limb—dinner in her claws.

Rain softens the world.
All night moon and fog.
All morning wet roses.

I love you.
The voice of flowers.

Tell Me If It's True

Haight St., San Francisco (2009)

Green-haired woman on red bike, speeding.
Skinhead on skateboard, speeding.
Untamed man stopping traffic,
walking down the middle of the street,
an oracle in several layers of coal-colored coats,
waving his arms and hollering at the darkening sky:
"You lose your shine, Ms. Moony Night?
Bring back Jesus in his prime
and jack open the clouds!"

Punk in leather jacket, big orange and white
Burger King patches sewn on the sleeves,
but two letters changed—Murder King.
He goes in Double Rainbow,
sits beside neon rainbow sign,
licks coconut-macadamia ice cream from a cup.

Woman in Wonder Woman mask
playing hopscotch, jumping on imaginary
squares, hopping, swaggering, saying,
"Now you see me, now you don't. Fuck off."

Bus pulls up to the curb. An old man wearing a
monocle, carrying a briefcase, climbs down,
presses a polka dot handkerchief to his brow,
and whispers to a world damn near deaf,
"Spare me, Lord. My wagon's been draggin' for sixty years."

Someone in the distance, more voice than substance,
says, "Close your eyes, whirl in a circle.
Whirl and whirl till there's no effort.
Now swing open your eyes.
Wait for stillness in the body,
in the bodies of others,
in the street,
the world, the sky,

and then—I mean now—
tell me if it's true:
"Wherever you turn, there is the face of God."

Equations

Love brings more love,
silence more song.

*En la pena,
en la alegría—
hay la madre,
hay el mar.*

Within pain,
within joy—
the mother,
the ocean.

Acknowledgements

My thanks to the editors of the following anthologies, in which the following poems first appeared.

In *The Zuni Mountain Poets*, edited by John Carter-North, Margaret Gross and Thomas Davis, "Privilege," "Altar," "Autumn Leaf," and "The Sea."

In *No More Can Fit Into the Evening, an Anthology of Diverse Voices*, edited by Thomas Davis and Standing Feather, "Morning," "Gravity," "Breathing Out," and "Long Distance Runners."

In "Settling My Estate," the third stanza is from Shakespeare's *Hamlet*: "I could be bounded in a nutshell and count myself king of infinite space if it were not that I have bad dreams."

The final line of the poem "Soldier Home (Albuquerque, 2011)" quotes Fyodor Dostoyevsky: "Two plus two is the beginning of death.

The final line of the poem "Tell Me If It's True" is from the Sufi traction: Wherever you turn, there is the face of God.

A deep bow of gratitude to Thomas and Ethel Davis, Kate Brown, Pati Hays, Penny Hyde, Jon Marshall, Jack North, Pam and Jon Pickens, Redwulf and Standing Feather, the Zuni Mountain Poets, and the Veteran Writers' Group led by Maxine Hong Kingston.

Praise for James Janko's Novels

"With its theme of prejudice, privilege and power in Midwest America, *What We Don't Talk About* by James Janko is a timely (given the present and pressing social issues of being Black in America) and a deftly crafted novel by an author with a genuine flair for revealing the dramatic in the mundane…"
—*Midwest Book Review*

What We Don't Talk About is an enticing work of fiction…As the title hints, the book deals with unspoken—indeed at times unspeakable—issues townspeople hardly whisper in public…The author's power of language will magnetize the reader throughout…"
—*Albuquerque Journal*

"Reading *What We Don't Talk About* is like looking inside a snow globe, and seeing a country town in America's heartland at Christmastime…Janko's miraculous writing connects…all of us to all others. Every good thing we do, and every bad, affects the whole world.
—Maxine Hong Kingston, author of *The Woman Warrior*

"Reading *The Clubhouse Thief* is akin to listening to a Gustav Mahler symphony. Mahler's symphonies have broad parallels to real life in the world; they meditate on nature, politics, religion, joy, death, suffering, identity, poetry, and literature…Janko's novel has the same type of broad parallels, using baseball as his modus operandi."
—*Windy City Reviews*

"The historic problem with sports fiction is that the fictional, internal dramas on display can't compare with what we read in the best of sports biography. But with James Janko's *The Clubhouse Thief*, we have sports fiction that rises to the level of art…An absolute triumph."
—Dave Zirin, author of *A People's History of Sports in the United States*

"Janko delivers a meditative and lyrical baseball novel… A spirited vision of America and its national game."
—*Kirkus Reviews*

"Nothing in the publisher's biography of James Janko suggests he is a poet, but his book [*Buffalo Boy and Geronimo*] is what used to be called, admiringly, 'a poet's novel.' Readers who seek a complex plot won't find it here, but the lives of the two antiheroes…are rendered in such rich textures that one sometimes feels Virginia Woolf is writing them."
   —Gerald Nicosia, *Los Angeles Times Book Review*

"An anti-war novel certainly, but very much its own kind…Folkloric in approach, it's sustained by prose that is often lyrical, though never self-conscious."
   —*Kirkus Reviews* (starred review)

"In a sense, nature can be considered the protagonist of Janko's novel, as well as its theme…*Buffalo Boy and Geronimo* suggests that spiritual communion with the universe will enable us to transcend our differences, be they political, racial, or societal. Janko's novel also implies that all life should be treated with dignity and respect, and it challenges us to worship the very ground upon which we tread."
   —*San Francisco Chronicle*

BIOGRAPHY

In 1969, James Janko was drafted into the Viet Nam War, which the Vietnamese call the American War. He refused to carry a weapon while serving as a combat medic in an infantry battalion commanded by Colonel George Armstrong Custer III. His medals include the Bronze Star for Valor, which he returned to the U.S. government in 1986 to protest their military involvement in Central America. In 2008, Janko gaveaway two medals. His Combat Medical Badge went to Tran Thi Hoan, a nineteen-year-old Vietnamese woman who was born without legs due to her mother's exposure to Agent Orange. He gave his Purple Heart to Dang Hong Nhut, who suffered from cancer due to her exposure to Agent Orange. Nhut died in 2017.

After his time in the war, Janko studied ecology at UC Berkeley and received a B.S. in Conservation of Natural Resources. He is a member of the Albuquerque chapter of Veterans for Peace and the Climate Crisis & Militarism Project of Veterans for Peace.

James Janko's most recent novel, *What We Don't Talk About*, was published by the University of Wisconsin Press in 2022. His novel, *The Clubhouse Thief* (2018*)*, won the Association of Writers and Writing Programs (AWP) Award for the Novel. His debut novel, *Buffalo Boy and Geronimo* (Northwestern University Press/ Curbstone), received wide critical acclaim and two awards: The Association of Asian American Studies Book Award and the Northern California Book Award. His novel, *The Wire-Walker*, was a finalist for the 2023 Donald L. Jordan Prize for Literary Excellence and was awarded the Juniper Prize by the University of Massachusetts Press. Excerpts of *The Wire-Walker* appeared in the Fall/Winter 2022 issue of *Nimrod International Journal*.

Janko's short stories have appeared in *The Massachusetts Review*, *The Sun*, *The Iowa Review*, and *Eureka Literary Magazine*, among others.

www.ingramcontent.com/pod-product-compliance
Lightning Source LLC
Chambersburg PA
CBHW051602010526
44118CB00023B/2796